CW00457845

INTERESTING
FACTS
2024

VOL. 1

1- The first computer virus was created in 1982 and was called the Elk Cloner.

2- Honey never spoils. Archaeologists have found pots of honey in ancient Egyptian tombs that are over 3,000 years old and still perfectly edible.

3- The average smartphone today has more computing power than the computers used for the Apollo 11 moon landing.

4- There are more possible iterations of a game of chess than there are atoms in the observable universe.

5- The city of Reykjavik, Iceland, is heated by geothermal energy, and about 87% of the country's homes are heated this way.

6- Alfred Hitchcock's "Rope" (1948) was filmed to look like one continuous take, although technological limitations at the time made this impossible.

7- Beethoven, one of the greatest composers of all time, continued to compose music even after he became deaf.

8- The Eiffel Tower can be 15 cm taller during the summer due to thermal expansion.

9- The ancient Olympic Games in Greece (776 BC to 393 AD) featured events such as chariot racing, wrestling, and the pentathlon.

10- The first computer programming language was Fortran, developed in the 1950s.

11- Space is not completely silent; it contains faint background noise known as the cosmic microwave background radiation.

12- The oldest known map is from ancient Babylon and dates back to the 6th century BC.

13- Greenland has the world's largest national park, Northeast Greenland National Park, which is larger than all but 29 countries.

14- The James Webb Space Telescope, set to launch in the future, is designed to be the successor to the Hubble Space Telescope.

15- The largest known galaxy is IC 1101, which is over six million light-years in diameter.

16- The first Apple computer, the Apple I, was sold for $666.66.

17- The movie "Titanic" was more expensive to make than the actual ship.

18- There are more than 8.7 million known species on Earth, but scientists...

estimate there could be up to 100 million more undiscovered species.

19- The word "science" comes from the Latin word "scientia," meaning knowledge.

20- Lake Victoria in Africa is the largest tropical lake in the world.

21- The first patent for the computer mouse was awarded to Douglas Engelbart and William English in 1970.

22- The famous shower scene in "Psycho" took seven days to shoot and consists of 77 different camera angles.

23- The Treaty of Versailles, signed in 1919, ended World War I and imposed harsh penalties on Germany.

24- Usain Bolt holds the record for the fastest 100m and 200m sprints in track and field.

25- The word "robot" comes from the Czech word "robota," which means forced labor.

26- The first World Series in baseball took place in 1903 between the Boston Red Sox and the Pittsburgh Pirates.

27- The first women's basketball game was played in 1892 at Smith College in Northampton, Massachusetts.

28- The first computer video game is widely considered to be "Spacewar!," created in 1962.

29- The term "Impressionism" was coined from the title of Claude Monet's painting "Impression, Sunrise."

30- The Strait of Gibraltar, which separates Europe from Africa, is only about 14 kilometers (8.7 miles) wide at its narrowest point.

31- The first recorded game of baseball was played in 1846 in Hoboken, New Jersey.

32- The Trans-Siberian Railway is the longest continuous railway in the world, connecting Moscow with Vladivostok, a distance of about 9,289 kilometers (5,772 miles).

33- The Seven Years' War (1756–1763) was a global conflict involving major European powers and is considered the first "world war."

34- The first successful video game console was the Magnavox Odyssey, released in 1972.

35- The first recorded art heist occurred in 1473 when two panels from a polyptych were stolen in Florence.

36- Cleopatra lived closer in time to the moon landing than to the construction of the Great Pyramid of Giza.

37- The Russian Revolution of 1917 marked the end of the Romanov dynasty and the beginning of the Soviet Union.

38- The first Wimbledon Championship was held in 1877, and only men were allowed to compete.

39- The Library of Alexandria, one of the largest and most significant libraries of the ancient world, was destroyed in a series of incidents over centuries.

40- The iconic "warp speed" effect in "Star Trek" was achieved by shaking the camera and zooming in simultaneously.

41- The first commercially available computer, the UNIVAC I, was delivered in 1951 and cost around $1.2 million.

42- The longest-running radio show in history is the Grand Ole Opry in...

Nashville, Tennessee, which has been on the air since 1925.

43- "The Persistence of Memory" by Salvador Dalí features melting clocks and is often interpreted as a meditation on the relativity of time.

44- The Magna Carta, signed in 1215, limited the power of the English monarchy and influenced the development of constitutional law.

45- The longest-running film in cinema history is "The Rocky Horror Picture Show," which has been in continuous release since 1975.

46- The world's smallest art masterpiece is a tiny engraving on a hair by micro-artist Willard Wigan.

47- The Mariana Trench in the western Pacific Ocean is the deepest part of the world's oceans, reaching a depth of about 36,070 feet (10,994 meters).

48- The first computer, the ENIAC, was completed in 1945 and weighed 27 tons.

49- The concept of a wormhole is a hypothetical tunnel-like structure that could connect two separate points in spacetime.

50- The code of Hammurabi, one of the earliest and most complete written legal codes, dates back to 1754 BC.

51- The longest tennis match in history lasted 11 hours and 5 minutes, played over three days at Wimbledon in 2010.

52- Neptune's moon Triton is unique because it orbits the planet in a retrograde direction, opposite to the planet's rotation.

53- The ancient Egyptians used a form of perspective in their art, often portraying the most important figures as the largest.

54- The Great Wall of galaxies is a massive structure of galaxies stretching over 500 million light-years across space.

55- There are more atoms in a single glass of water than there are glasses of water in all the oceans on Earth.

56- The speed of a computer mouse is measured in "Mickeys."

57- The light from the Sun takes about 8 minutes and 20 seconds to reach Earth.

58- Badminton is the fastest racquet sport, with shuttlecocks reaching speeds of over 200 mph.

59- The Academy Awards, also known as the Oscars, were first held in 1929, and tickets cost just $5.

60- The first computer programmer was Ada Lovelace, who wrote the first algorithm intended for implementation...

on Charles Babbage's Analytical Engine in the mid-1800s.

61- Golf is the only sport to have been played on the moon. Alan Shepard hit a golf ball with a makeshift club during the Apollo 14 mission.

62- The smell of rain is caused by a bacteria called actinomycetes.

63- The French Revolution, which began in 1789, led to the rise of Napoleon Bonaparte and the end of the monarchy.

64- The movie "Casablanca" was shot entirely on set, with no scenes filmed in the actual city of Casablanca.

65- The human brain is more active during the night than the day.

66- The first photo uploaded to the internet was of a comedy band called "Les Horribles Cernettes."

67- Space is constantly expanding, and galaxies are moving away from each other due to the expansion of the universe.

68- The Dead Sea, bordered by Jordan and Israel, is so salty that you can effortlessly float on its surface.

69- The shortest-reigning monarch in history was Louis-Antoine of France, who became king for just 20 minutes in 1830.

70- The concept of a music video was popularized by MTV in the 1980s.

71- Antarctica is the driest and windiest continent on Earth.

72- The largest asteroid in the asteroid belt between Mars and Jupiter is Ceres, which is also classified as a dwarf planet.

73- The largest desert in the world is Antarctica, as deserts are defined by...

low precipitation, not necessarily high temperatures.

74- The concept of zero was invented by the ancient Indians.

75- The term "hackathon" is a portmanteau of "hack" and "marathon" and refers to collaborative software development events.

76- "Starry Night" by Vincent van Gogh depicts the view from his asylum room and is known for its swirling night sky.

77- The largest moon in the solar system is Ganymede, a moon of Jupiter.

78- The ancient Greeks believed that art was a form of mimesis, the imitation of nature.

79- The art movement known as "Fauvism" emphasized bold color and brushwork, with Henri Matisse as one of its key figures.

80- Cows have best friends and can become stressed when they are separated.

81- The French explorer Jacques Cartier claimed Canada for France in 1534.

82- The "Birth of Venus" by Sandro Botticelli is a famous painting depicting the goddess Venus emerging from the sea.

83- The first official international cricket match was played between the United States and Canada in 1844.

84- The speed of light is approximately 299,792 kilometers per second.

85- The island of Madagascar, located off the southeastern coast of Africa, is home to unique plant and animal species found nowhere else on Earth.

86- The speed of light is approximately 299,792 kilometers per second (186,282 miles per second).

87- The Eiffel Tower was initially criticized by some of France's leading artists and intellectuals when it was built in 1889.

88- The Tropic of Cancer and the Tropic of Capricorn are imaginary lines that mark the northernmost and southernmost points where the sun appears directly overhead.

89- The Great Red Spot on Jupiter is a massive storm that has been raging for at least 350 years.

90- The largest known exoplanet is Kepler-39b, which is about 18 times the mass of Jupiter.

91- The concept of the World Wide Web was proposed by Sir Tim Berners-Lee in 1989.

92- Space is not truly black; it has a faint glow known as the "cosmic optical background."

93- The 1980s saw the rise of the compact disc (CD), which could hold 74 minutes of music. This length was chosen to accommodate Beethoven's 9th Symphony.

94- The use of perspective in art was popularized during the Renaissance, notably by artists like Brunelleschi and Alberti.

95- The Darien Gap, a dense and impassable jungle between Panama and Colombia, is the only break in the Pan-American Highway.

96- The term "captcha" stands for "Completely Automated Public Turing test to tell Computers and Humans Apart."

97- The first Winter Olympic Games were held in Chamonix, France, in 1924.

98- The smell of freshly-cut grass is actually a plant distress call.

99- The first recorded women's soccer game took place in 1892 in Glasgow, Scotland.

100- The African continent is the only continent situated in all four hemispheres: Northern, Southern, Eastern, and Western.

101- The Earth is about 4.54 billion years old.

102- The first camera phone was released by J-Phone in Japan in 2000.

103- Jupiter is so large that it could fit over 1,300 Earths inside.

104- The Dead Sea Scrolls, some of the oldest known biblical manuscripts ...

were discovered in the Qumran Caves near the Dead Sea.

105- The average person walks the equivalent of five times around the world in their lifetime.

106- The term "Bluetooth" is named after a 10th-century Danish king, Harald "Bluetooth" Gormsson.

107- The largest number of participants in a single marathon is over 110,000, set in the 2016 Beijing Marathon.

108- The ancient city of Carthage was famously destroyed by the Romans during the Punic Wars.

109- The first domain name ever registered was symbolics.com on March 15, 1985.

110- The first commercial cell phone, the Motorola DynaTAC 8000x, was released in 1983 and weighed 2.2 pounds.

111- The hottest planet in our solar system is Venus, with an average surface temperature of about 465 degrees Celsius (869 degrees Fahrenheit).

112- The fastest goal in soccer history was scored in 1.8 seconds by Hakan Şükür in 2002.

113- The first search engine, Archie, was created in 1990.

114- The modern bicycle used in cycling races was first developed in the 19th century.

115- The first recorded use of shin guards in soccer was in 1874 by Sam Weller Widdowson.

116- "Les Demoiselles d'Avignon" by Pablo Picasso is a groundbreaking work that is considered a precursor to Cubism.

117- The surrealist artist René Magritte is famous for his painting "The Treachery of Images," with the caption "This is not a pipe."

118- The concept of 3D printing was first introduced in the 1980s by Chuck Hull.

119- The Beatles used the word "love" 613 times in their songs.

120- The QR code was invented in 1994 by Masahiro Hara, an engineer at the Japanese company Denso Wave.

121- The highest-scoring soccer game in history ended 149-0, with Stade Olympique de L'emyrne defeating AS Adema in 2002. However, AS Adema scored all the goals, as Stade Olympique de L'emyrne deliberately scored own goals to protest a refereeing decision.

122- Stanley Kubrick's "The Shining" holds the record for the most retakes of a...

22

single scene, with the baseball bat scene requiring 127 takes.

123- The Milky Way galaxy is part of a local group of galaxies that includes the Andromeda Galaxy.

124- A teaspoonful of a neutron star would weigh about 6 billion tons on Earth due to its extreme density.

125- Every year, the Moon moves about 3.8 centimeters away from the Earth.

126- The Aztecs used cocoa beans as a form of currency.

127- The word "scientist" was first coined by William Whewell in 1833.

128- The Ming Dynasty built the Great Wall of China to protect against invasions from the north.

129- Frida Kahlo, a Mexican artist, is known for her self-portraits that often...

incorporated symbolic elements from her life.

130- The word "nerd" was first coined by Dr. Seuss in "If I Ran the Zoo" in 1950.

131- A day on Venus is longer than a year on Venus. It takes about 243 Earth days for Venus to complete one rotation on its axis, but only about 225 Earth days to orbit the Sun.

132- The human eye can distinguish about 10 million different colors.

133- The highest-scoring NBA game ended in a 186-184 victory for the Detroit Pistons over the Denver Nuggets in 1983.

134- The country with the most islands is Sweden, boasting over 267,000 islands.

135- The first known use of biological warfare occurred in 1346 when Mongols catapulted plague-infected corpses into the Crimean city of Caffa.

136- The Battle of Hastings in 1066 marked the Norman conquest of England.

137- The largest volcano in the solar system is Olympus Mons on Mars, which is about 13.6 miles (22 kilometers) high.

138- The Battle of Marathon in 490 BC is famous for the marathon race, inspired by a messenger running 26.2 miles to Athens to announce the victory.

139- The first computer programmer was Ada Lovelace, who wrote the first algorithm intended for implementation on Charles Babbage's analytical engine.

140- The first organized hockey game was played in Montreal in 1875.

141- The Caspian Sea, bordered by five countries, is the largest enclosed inland body of water on Earth.

142- Mozart was composing music by the age of five, and he wrote his first symphony at the age of eight.

143- The Guinness World Record for the most people playing the same piano simultaneously is 88, set in Germany.

144- The world's largest volcano is Mauna Loa in Hawaii.

145- The Great Emu War was a failed attempt by Australia to curb the population of emus in 1932.

146- The Karakoram Highway, connecting Pakistan and China, is the highest paved international road in the world.

147- The concept of "augmented reality" (AR) involves integrating digital information into the user's real-world environment.

148- A year on Mercury is only about 88 Earth days, but a day on Mercury (one rotation on its axis) takes about 59 Earth days.

149- The Silk Road facilitated trade and cultural exchange between the East and West for centuries.

150- The Himalayas are home to the world's highest concentration of peaks over 26,247 feet (8,000 meters) high.

151- Vincent van Gogh only sold one painting during his lifetime, "The Red Vineyard."

152- Iceland is known as the "Land of Fire and Ice" due to its combination of glaciers and volcanoes.

153- The word "robot" comes from the Czech word "robota," meaning forced labor.

154- The term "Renaissance" means "rebirth" in French and refers to the period of renewed interest in art and learning in Europe from the 14th to the 17th century.

155- The word "symphony" comes from the Greek word "symphonia," which means "sounding together."

156- The concept of the Internet of Things (IoT) refers to the interconnectivity of everyday objects through the internet.

157- The Ural Mountains in Russia are considered the natural boundary between Europe and Asia.

158- The closest galaxy to the Milky Way is the Andromeda Galaxy, located about 2.5 million light-years away.

159- The world's highest waterfall, Angel Falls, is located in Venezuela and drops water from a height of 3,212 feet (979 meters).

160- The Battle of Gettysburg was a turning point in the American Civil War, fought from July 1 to 3, 1863.

161- The concept of a "white hole" is a theoretical region of space-time that emits energy, but nothing can enter it.

162- The first Super Bowl was played in 1967 between the Green Bay Packers and the Kansas City Chiefs.

163- The world's most extensive collection of art is in the Vatican Museums, containing over 70,000 works.

164- The Neolithic Revolution, around 10,000 BC, marked the transition from hunter-gatherer societies to agriculture-based civilizations.

165- The first successful open-heart surgery was performed by Dr. Daniel Hale Williams in 1893.

166- The world's largest archipelago is Indonesia, consisting of over 17,000 islands.

167- The "Wilhelm Scream" is a stock sound effect used in over 400 films, starting in 1951.

168- The Battle of Stalingrad in 1942-1943 was one of the bloodiest battles in history and a turning point in World War II.

169- The Voyager 1 spacecraft carries a golden record with sounds and images representing Earth, intended for any extraterrestrial intelligence that may encounter it.

170- The sound of the velociraptors in "Jurassic Park" was created by blending the sounds of tortoises mating and a walrus bellowing.

171- The longest film ever made is "Logistics" (2012), with a runtime of 35 days.

172- The concept of virtual reality dates back to the 1960s, but it became more widely known in the 1990s.

173- The Amazon Rainforest produces 20% of the world's oxygen.

174- Honeybees can recognize human faces.

175- The Great Wave off Kanagawa, a woodblock print by Hokusai, is one of the most iconic images in Japanese art.

176- The closest galaxy cluster to the Milky Way is the Virgo Cluster, located about 54 million light-years away.

177- The smell of gasoline is intentionally added to it for safety reasons; otherwise, it is odorless.

178- The game of chess is considered a sport by the International Olympic Committee.

179- The highest-grossing film of all time (as of 2023) is "Avatar," directed by James Cameron, with $2,923,706,026.

180- The term "Wi-Fi" doesn't actually stand for anything. It is just a trademarked term.

181- The "Girl with a Pearl Earring" by Johannes Vermeer is often referred to as the "Mona Lisa of the North."

182- Saturn's rings are made up of countless icy particles, ranging in size from tiny grains to several meters in diameter.

183- The world's largest music festival is Summerfest in Milwaukee, USA, attracting over 800,000 attendees annually.

184- The Galápagos Islands inspired Charles Darwin's theory of evolution by natural selection.

185- The term "Gothic" in art originally referred to the Goths, a Germanic tribe, but later became associated with a style of architecture and art.

186- Vincent van Gogh created over 2,000 works of art, including around 900 paintings and 1,100 drawings, in just over a decade.

187- Yoko Ono's art installation "Cut Piece" involves her sitting on a stage while audience members cut away pieces of her clothing.

188- The term "avant-garde" in art refers to innovative and experimental works that push the boundaries of traditional artistic styles.

189- A day on Venus is longer than a year on Venus. It takes about 243 Earth...

days for Venus to complete one rotation on its axis.

190- A group of flamingos is called a "flamboyance."

191- The term "bug" in computer science originated when a moth caused a malfunction in the Mark II computer in 1947.

192- The Trojan Horse was a wooden horse used by the Greeks during the Trojan War to infiltrate the city of Troy.

193- The word "piano" is an abbreviation of the full Italian name for the instrument, "pianoforte," which means "soft-loud."

194- "Guernica," a powerful anti-war painting by Pablo Picasso, was created in response to the bombing of a Spanish town during the Spanish Civil War.

195- The term "robot" was first coined by Czech writer Karel Čapek in his 1920...

play "R.U.R.," standing for "Rossum's Universal Robots."

196- The largest known star is UY Scuti, with a diameter estimated to be over 1,700 times that of the Sun.

197- The Great Ocean Road in Australia is the world's longest war memorial, built by returned servicemen after World War I.

198- The term "blog" is a contraction of "web log" and was coined in 1997.

199- The shortest war in history was between Britain and Zanzibar on August 27, 1896. Zanzibar surrendered after 38 minutes.

200- The first World Cup of soccer was held in 1930 in Uruguay.

201- Michelangelo's iconic statue, David, stands at 17 feet tall and was carved from a single block of marble.

202- Lake Titicaca, located on the border of Peru and Bolivia, is the highest navigable lake in the world.

203- The first successful vaccine was developed by Edward Jenner in 1796 for smallpox.

204- The Atacama Desert in Chile is one of the driest places on Earth, with some weather stations recording years without rainfall.

205- The first modern Olympic Games were held in Athens in 1896, featuring 13 countries and 43 events.

206- The term "disc jockey" was first coined by radio announcer Walter Winchell in 1935.

207- The first recorded instance of a musical instrument being played in space was an Australian didgeridoo on the space shuttle Endeavour in 1993.

208- A single raindrop can fall at speeds of up to 22 miles per hour.

209- The first successful transatlantic telegraph cable was laid in 1858, connecting North America and Europe.

210- The world's largest guitar ensemble consisted of 7,346 participants and took place in Poland.

211- The Olympic flame is lit using the sun's rays in Olympia, Greece, and then travels to the host city for the Games.

212- The Great Barrier Reef, off the coast of Australia, is the largest coral reef system in the world.

213- The first digital camera was created by Kodak engineer Steven Sasson in 1975.

214- The island of New Guinea is home to the third-largest rainforest in the world after the Amazon and Congo rainforests.

215- Pablo Picasso, one of the most influential artists of the 20th century, co-founded the Cubist movement.

216- The Earth's core is as hot as the surface of the sun.

217- The Spanish Inquisition lasted for nearly 350 years, from 1478 to 1834.

218- The coldest temperature ever recorded on Earth was -128.6°F (-89.2°C) in Antarctica.

219- The record for the most takes in a single scene goes to "The 40-Year-Old Virgin," where Paul Rudd and Seth Rogen couldn't stop laughing, resulting in 160 takes.

220- The first computer mouse was invented by Doug Engelbart in 1964, and it was made of wood.

221- The first recorded Olympic Games took place in 776 BC in Olympia, Greece.

222- The world record for the most push-ups in one hour is 2,220, set by Charles Servizio in 1993.

223- The Great Victoria Desert in Australia is the largest desert on the Australian continent.

224- The first documented game of American football was played between Princeton and Rutgers in 1869.

225- The movie "Psycho" (1960) was the first American film to show a toilet flushing on screen.

226- The first film to win an Academy Award for Best Picture was "Wings" in 1929.

227- In 2016, the Chicago Cubs won the World Series for the first time in 108 years.

228- The first successful human heart transplant was performed by Dr. Christiaan Barnard in South Africa in 1967.

229- The first electronic digital computer, the Atanasoff-Berry Computer (ABC), was completed in 1942.

230- The first mobile phone call was made in 1973 by Martin Cooper, a Motorola executive.

231- The world's largest desert is Antarctica.

232- The "Mona Lisa" has its own mailbox at the Louvre because of the countless love letters and notes it receives.

233- Karate will make its debut as an Olympic sport in the 2020 Tokyo Games.

234- Space is not completely empty; it contains a very low density of particles, including atoms, ions, and cosmic dust.

235- The Sun's core temperature is about 15 million degrees Celsius (27 million degrees Fahrenheit).

236- The first photograph ever taken was by Joseph Nicéphore Niépce in 1826, titled "View from the Window at Le Gras."

237- The first music streaming service, called "Internet Underground Music Archive" (IUMA), was launched in 1993.

238- The first computer mouse sold commercially was the Xerox 8010 Star Information System in 1981.

239- The "Happy Birthday" song is still under copyright protection, and its use...

in public performances requires payment of royalties.

240- The world's first recorded song was "Au Clair de la Lune," recorded in 1860.

241- The concept of the computer "firewall" was first introduced in the 1980s to protect networks from unauthorized access.

242- The first cloned mammal was a sheep named Dolly, born in 1996.

243- The first official game of ice hockey was played in 1875 in Montreal.

244- The term "sculpture" comes from the Latin word "sculptura," meaning "carving."

245- The earliest form of paper was invented by the ancient Egyptians around 3000 BC.

246- The ancient Egyptians used honey as a form of currency.

247- The term "blockbuster" originated from World War II, referring to a bomb powerful enough to destroy a city block.

248- The industrial revolution, marking the transition to new manufacturing processes, began in the late 18th century.

249- The world record for the longest golf drive is 515 yards, set by Mike Austin in 1974.

250- Jupiter has a powerful magnetic field, more than ten times stronger than any other planet in our solar system.

251- The word "quarantine" comes from the Italian words "quaranta giorni," meaning 40 days, which was the period that ships were required to be isolated during the Black Death.

252- Lake Baikal in Siberia is the deepest lake in the world, reaching a depth of about 5,387 feet (1,642 meters).

253- The Milky Way is on a collision course with the Andromeda Galaxy, and they are expected to collide in about 4 billion years.

254- The largest volcano on Earth is Mauna Loa in Hawaii, but it is dwarfed by some of the volcanoes on Mars.

255- The oldest known cave paintings date back to around 40,000 years ago and were discovered in Indonesia.

256- The Maldives, an island nation in the Indian Ocean, is the flattest country on Earth, with no point more than 2.4 meters (7 feet 10 inches) above sea level.

257- The word "nerd" was first coined by Dr. Seuss in "If I Ran the Zoo" in 1950.

258- The human body has more bacterial cells than human cells.

259- The Treaty of Westphalia in 1648 ended the Thirty Years' War and is considered a foundation of modern diplomacy.

260- The first computer virus for Microsoft DOS was Brain, created in 1986.

261- The first video game, "Tennis for Two," was created in 1958.

262- Black holes can bend and distort light, creating gravitational lensing effects.

263- The first photo ever taken was in 1826 by Joseph Nicéphore Niépce.

264- The International Space Station (ISS) travels at an average speed of about 28,000 kilometers per hour (17,500 miles per hour).

265- The edge of space is not precisely defined but is often considered to be around 100 kilometers (62 miles) above Earth's surface, known as the Kármán line.

266- The longest recorded time between two twins being born is 87 days.

267- One year on Pluto is equivalent to about 248 Earth years.

268- The Great Wall of China is not visible from the moon without aid.

269- The first 1TB hard drive was released by Seagate in 2007.

270- Mount Kilimanjaro in Tanzania is the tallest freestanding mountain in the world.

271- The highest score ever recorded in a single game of basketball is 186 points, set in 1983 in a game between Detroit and Denver.

272- The Danakil Depression in Ethiopia is one of the hottest places on Earth, with temperatures reaching up to 145 degrees Fahrenheit (63 degrees Celsius).

273- The first public screening of a movie took place in Paris in 1895, with the Lumière brothers' Cinématographe.

274- The record for the fastest serve in tennis is 163.7 mph, achieved by Novak Djokovic in 2022.

275- The city of Istanbul, Turkey, is the only city in the world that straddles two continents: Europe and Asia.

276- The Mayans used a complex writing system known as hieroglyphics.

277- The QWERTY keyboard layout was designed in 1873 for typewriters and is still widely used today.

278- The first film with a 3D sequence was "Bwana Devil" in 1952.

279- The concept of the emoji originated in Japan in the late 1990s.

280- The "Thinker" by Auguste Rodin is part of a larger work called "The Gates of Hell" and represents Dante Alighieri contemplating his epic poem "Divine Comedy."

281- A teaspoonful of neutron star material would weigh about six billion tons on Earth.

282- The Great Fire of London in 1666 destroyed much of the city, but only six people were recorded to have died.

283- The first recorded use of the term "home run" in baseball was in 1856.

284- The Great Famine in Ireland from 1845 to 1852 led to the deaths of...

approximately one million people and mass emigration.

285- The term "pop art" originated in the mid-20th century and is associated with artists like Andy Warhol and Roy Lichtenstein.

286- The didgeridoo, an Australian Aboriginal instrument, is one of the oldest musical instruments in the world, estimated to be over 1,500 years old.

287- The world's largest art museum is the State Hermitage Museum in St. Petersburg, Russia.

288- The RMS Titanic sank on its maiden voyage in 1912, resulting in the deaths of over 1,500 people.

289- An adult human is made up of approximately 7,000,000,000,000,000,000,000,000,000 (7 octillion) atoms.

290- The Cold War, a geopolitical tension between the United States and the Soviet Union, lasted from the end of World War II to the early 1990s.

291- The Moon is gradually moving away from Earth at a rate of about 3.8 centimeters (1.5 inches) per year.

292- The electric guitar was invented in 1931 by George Beauchamp and Adolph Rickenbacker.

293- There are more stars in the observable universe than there are grains of sand on all the beaches on Earth.

294- The fastest marathon ever run is 2 hours, 1 minute, and 39 seconds, achieved by Eliud Kipchoge in 2018.

295- The Gobi Desert in Asia is known for its extreme temperatures, ranging from -40 degrees Fahrenheit (-40 degrees Celsius) in winter to 122 degrees...

Fahrenheit (50 degrees Celsius) in summer.

296- The ancient Greeks had a word, "techne," encompassing both art and craft, reflecting their holistic view of creativity.

297- The longest-running radio show in the world is the Grand Ole Opry in Nashville, Tennessee, which has been on the air since 1925.

298- The term "iconography" refers to the study of visual symbols and their meaning in art.

299- The first color feature film was "Becky Sharp" in 1935, using the two-color Technicolor process.

300- The Bermuda Triangle, a loosely defined region in the western part of the North Atlantic Ocean, is known for the mysterious disappearance of ships and aircraft.

301- Banksy, a street artist whose identity remains unknown, is famous for his politically charged and satirical works.

302- The first email was sent by Ray Tomlinson in 1971, and it simply said "QWERTYUIOP."

303- The phrase "show business" comes from the entertainment district in New York known as the "Tenderloin," where theaters and brothels were concentrated.

304- Basketball was invented by Dr. James Naismith in 1891, who used peach baskets as goals.

305- The concept of the "Goldilocks Zone" refers to the habitable zone around a star where conditions are suitable for liquid water to exist on a planet's surface.

306- The first recorded instance of a sport was in 3000 BC in Egypt, where wrestling was depicted in a tomb.

307- The first music video ever played on MTV was "Video Killed the Radio Star" by The Buggles.

308- The construction of the Great Pyramids of Giza began around 2580 BC.

309- The term "cyberspace" was coined by science fiction writer William Gibson in his novel "Neuromancer."

310- The Pacific Ocean covers more area than all the landmasses combined.

311- The Sun makes up about 99.86% of the total mass of our solar system.

312- The Hundred Years' War between England and France actually lasted 116 years, from 1337 to 1453.

313- Hieronymus Bosch's painting "The Garden of Earthly Delights" is a triptych that depicts heaven, earth, and hell in intricate detail.

314- Octopuses have three hearts and blue blood.

315- Space is not a perfect vacuum; it contains very low-density particles, primarily in the form of gas and dust.

316- The highest score ever achieved in a single game of bowling is 300, a perfect game.

317- Canada has more lakes than the rest of the world combined.

318- Mount Everest, the world's tallest mountain, is still growing at a rate of about 4 millimeters per year.

319- The first recorded rules for modern water polo were established in 1877 in London.

320- The city of Rome is the only city in the world to have its own country entirely within it, the Vatican City.

321- The song "Jingle Bells" was originally written for Thanksgiving, not Christmas.

322- The average golf ball has 336 dimples.

323- The Nile River is the longest river in the world, stretching over 6,650 kilometers (4,130 miles).

324- The first organized marathon race was held during the 1896 Athens Olympics, inspired by the legend of Pheidippides.

325- Space is not completely silent; there are various sounds in space, including electromagnetic vibrations converted into sound waves.

326- Freddie Mercury designed the Queen logo himself, which features the zodiac signs of all four members.

327- The world's longest concert lasted for 639 hours and took place in a church in Germany.

328- The first human-made object to reach interstellar space is the Voyager 1 spacecraft, launched in 1977.

329- The first successful sustained powered flight was achieved by the Wright brothers in 1903.

330- The Great Depression, a severe worldwide economic depression, lasted from 1929 to the late 1930s.

331- Michael Phelps holds the record for the most Olympic gold medals won in a single Olympics, with eight in the 2008 Beijing Games.

332- The Rosetta Stone played a crucial role in deciphering ancient Egyptian hieroglyphs.

333- The Appalachian Mountains in North America are one of the oldest mountain ranges in the world.

334- The first computer with a graphical user interface (GUI) was the Xerox Alto, developed in 1973.

335- The character of Hannibal Lecter has been portrayed by three different actors who all won Academy Awards for their performances: Anthony Hopkins, Brian Cox, and Jodie Foster.

336- Cricket is one of the oldest known team sports, with records dating back to the 16th century.

337- The artist Yves Klein patented his own shade of blue called International Klein Blue (IKB).

338- The concept of the computer mouse was inspired by the cursor-arrow movement on early graphical user interfaces.

339- The Tour de France, one of the most famous cycling races, began in 1903.

340- The Black Death, one of the deadliest pandemics in human history, wiped out an estimated 75-200 million people in the 14th century.

341- The first 1GB hard drive was announced by IBM in 1980 and weighed about 550 pounds.

342- The most common element in the universe is hydrogen.

343- The closest black hole to Earth is likely in the constellation Vela, about 1,000 light-years away.

344- The world's first webcam was invented at the University of Cambridge to monitor a coffee pot.

345- The ozone layer is mainly found in the stratosphere and protects life on Earth by absorbing the majority of the sun's harmful ultraviolet radiation.

346- Jackson Pollock, a leading figure in the abstract expressionist movement, was known for his "drip paintings."

347- A single rainforest can produce 20% of the world's oxygen.

348- The word "canvas" originally referred to a type of fabric made from hemp used by artists for painting.

349- Russia spans 11 time zones, making it the country with the most time zones.

350- The Great Dividing Range in Australia is one of the longest mountain ranges in the world.

351- The largest volcano in our solar system, Olympus Mons on Mars, is about 13.6 miles (22 kilometers) high.

352- The fall of the Roman Empire is traditionally dated to 476 AD when the last Roman emperor, Romulus Augustulus, was deposed by the Germanic chieftain Odoacer.

353- The Hubble Space Telescope can see objects as far as 13.4 billion light-years away.

354- The longest continuous scientific experiment is the pitch drop experiment, started in 1927, which measures the flow of a piece of pitch over time.

355- The concept of dark matter is proposed to explain the gravitational effects observed in the universe, although its nature remains unknown.

356- The first ATM (Automated Teller Machine) was installed in 1967 by Barclays Bank in London.

357- The Berlin Wall, which divided East and West Berlin, fell in 1989, leading to the reunification of Germany.

358- The Maldives is the lowest country in the world, with an average ground level of 1.5 meters (4 feet 11 inches) above sea level.

359- The average person spends about 18% of their waking hours listening to music.

360- The first computer animated feature film was "Toy Story," released by Pixar in 1995.

361- Table tennis originated in England in the late 19th century as an after-dinner parlor game.

362- The first website ever created is still online. It was launched by Tim Berners-Lee in 1991.

363- The ancient city of Pompeii was preserved in ash after the eruption of Mount Vesuvius in 79 AD.

364- The Milky Way galaxy is thought to contain about 100 billion stars.

365- The ancient Chinese art form of paper cutting, or "jianzhi," dates back over 1,500 years.

366- The most expensive sports stadium ever built is the MetLife Stadium in New Jersey, costing over $1.6 billion.